LET'S FIND OUT ABOUT

THE MOON

by MARTHA AND CHARLES SHAPP

Pictures by Yukio Tashiro

FRANKLIN WATTS, INC.
575 Lexington Avenue, New York, N. Y. 10022

LET'S FIND OUT ABOUT THE MOON

The moon is our nearest neighbor in space.
It seems bigger and brighter than the stars but
   really is much smaller.
It seems bigger because it is so much closer to
   us than any star.
The moon travels around the earth just as the
   earth travels around the sun.

People have always been interested in the moon.
But long, long ago, people had no way to find
   out about the moon.
They just looked at it and wondered about it.
Then the telescope was invented.
Scientists were able to study the moon through
   telescopes and they learned many things.

In the last few years rockets have been sent to
the moon.
Some of these rockets have sent back pictures of
the moon.
Scientists now know a great deal about the
moon.
But they want to know more.

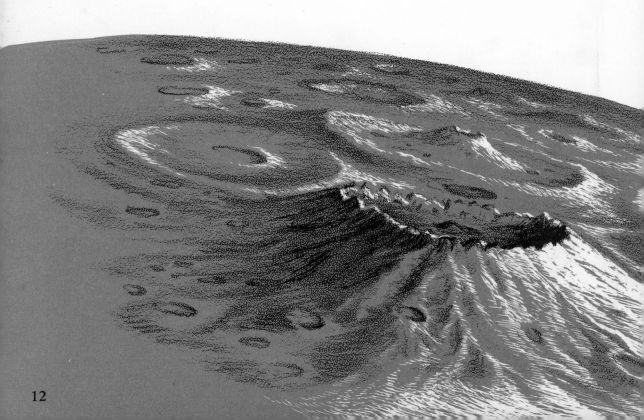

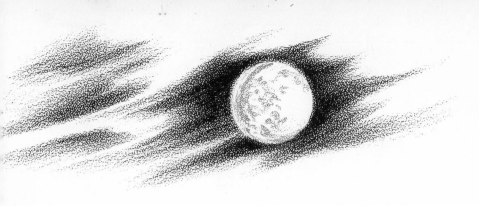

The best way to find out more is for someone
   to go and see.
So the scientists are getting ready to blast off
   a rocket that will land men on the moon.

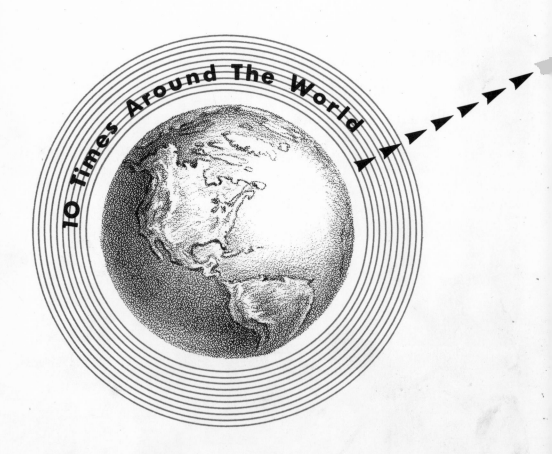

10 Times Around The World

240,000 MILES

What a difficult and dangerous trip that is
    going to be!
Although the moon is closer to us than any of
    the stars, it isn't really very close.
The moon is about 240,000 miles away from
    our earth.
This is almost ten times the distance around
    our earth.

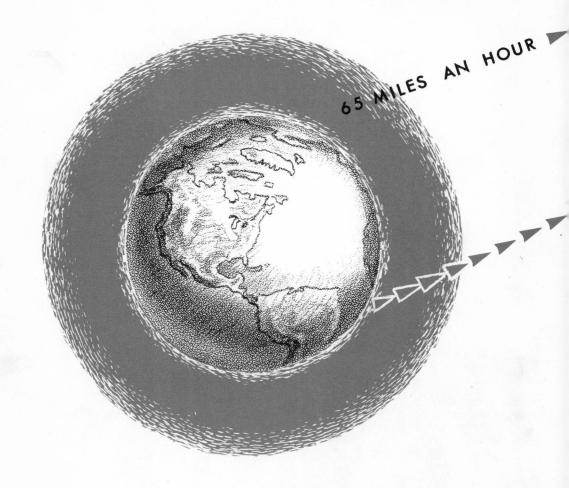

65 MILES AN HOUR

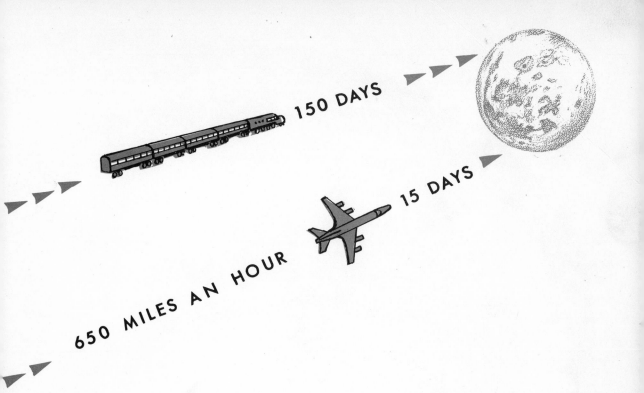

150 DAYS

15 DAYS

650 MILES AN HOUR

A train speeding day and night at 65 miles an
   hour would take about 150 days for the trip.
This is about five months.
A jet plane speeding day and night at 650
   miles an hour would take about 15 days.

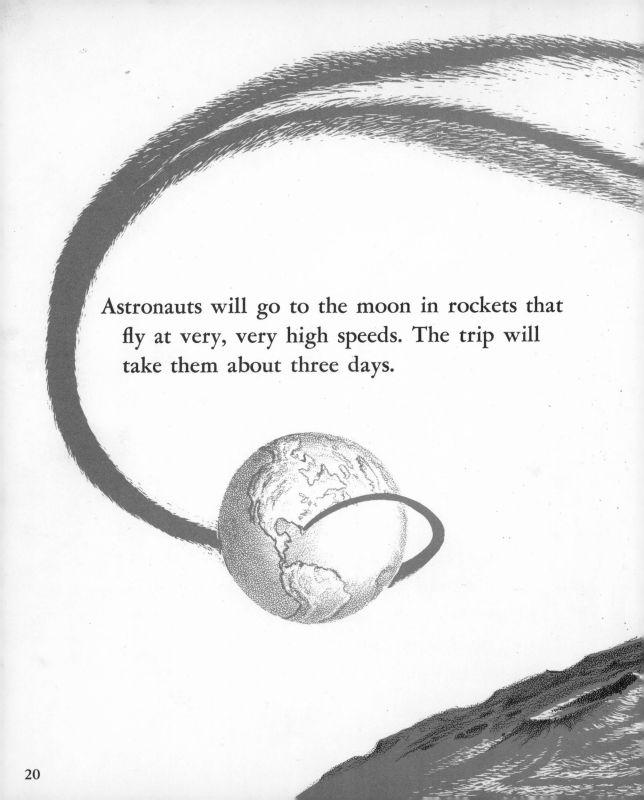

Astronauts will go to the moon in rockets that fly at very, very high speeds. The trip will take them about three days.

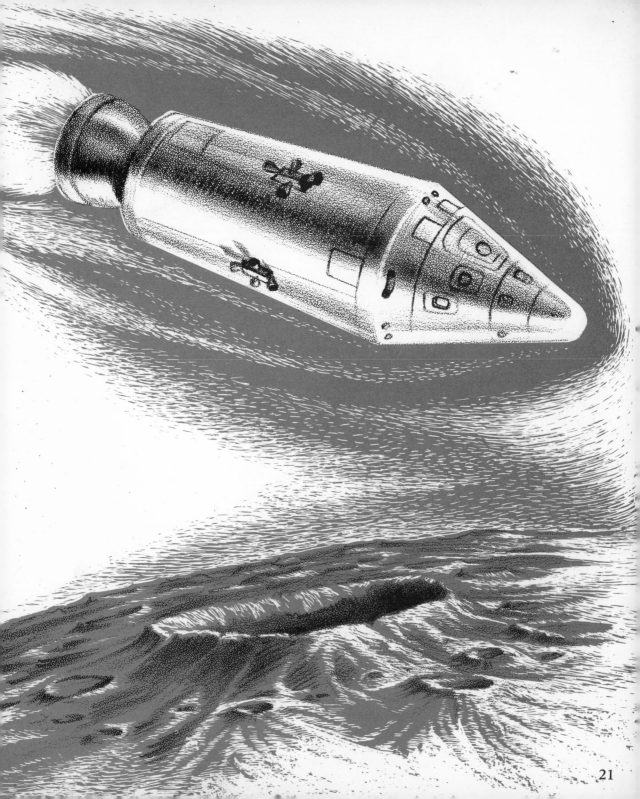

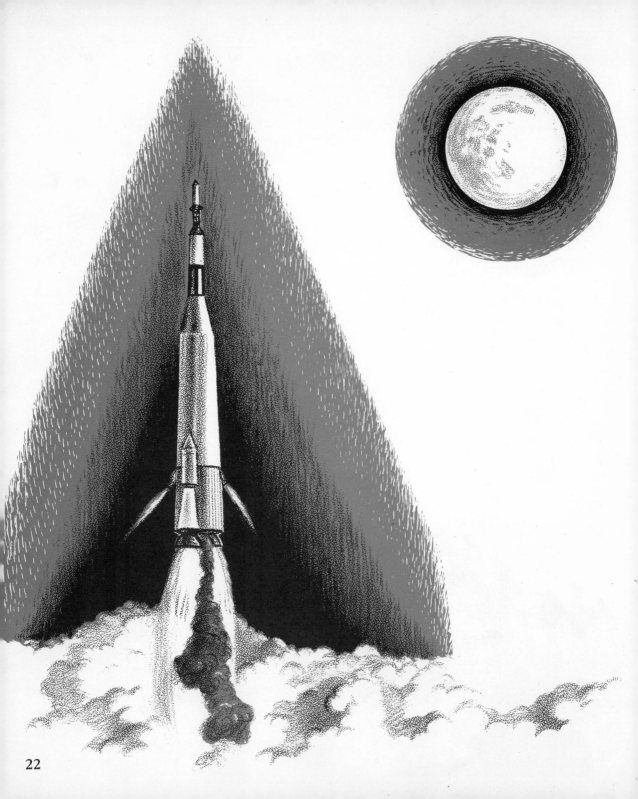

The moon rockets must be aimed from here on
  earth.
Imagine aiming at a target 240,000 miles away!
And that target is quite small.
If the earth were the size of a basketball, the
  moon would be the size of a tennis ball.

EARTH

MOON

2,300 MILES AN HOUR

And not only is the moon a small target to hit,
it is a moving target.
The moon circles around the earth at a speed
of about 2,300 miles an hour.
It takes the moon about a month to go once
around the earth.

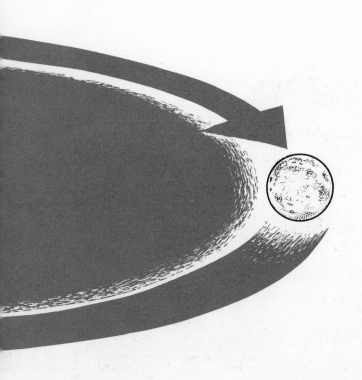

When the astronauts land on the moon, what
    will they find?
They will find a silent, dead world.
They will see high, jagged mountains and deep,
    deep holes called craters.
The astronauts will need special machines to
    travel over this rough surface.

The astronauts will find no water on the moon.
People cannot live without water.
The astronauts will have to bring water from
    the earth.

The astronauts will find no air on the moon.
People need air to breathe.
The astronauts will have to bring a supply of air.
They will have to carry air tanks with them all
the time.

The astronauts will find the moon a very silent
   place.
They will not hear a sound.
Sound is carried by air.
Since there is no air on the moon, there is no
   sound.
How will the astronauts talk to each other?
They will have to talk through radios.
Radio waves can travel without air.

There are days and nights on the moon.
But each day and each night is two weeks long.
During the two weeks of daytime the heat is so
    great that human beings could not live.
The astronauts working in the daytime on the
    moon would need cooling systems built into
    their clothes.

During the two weeks of night on the moon it
is so cold that a man would quickly freeze to
death.
To go out into the night, an astronaut would
need a heating system built into his clothes.

The force of gravity on the moon is weaker
than it is on earth.
This means that things are lighter on the moon
than they are on earth.
If you weigh 60 pounds on earth, you would
weigh only 10 pounds on the moon.
If you can jump four feet on earth, you would
be able to jump 24 feet on the moon.

How does the moon look to us here on earth?
It looks like a big, shiny ball.
But the moon does not shine with its own light.
The moon gets its light from the sun just as
the earth does.

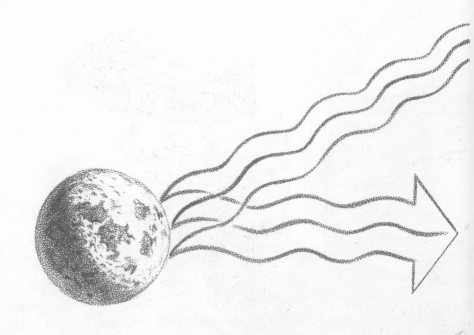

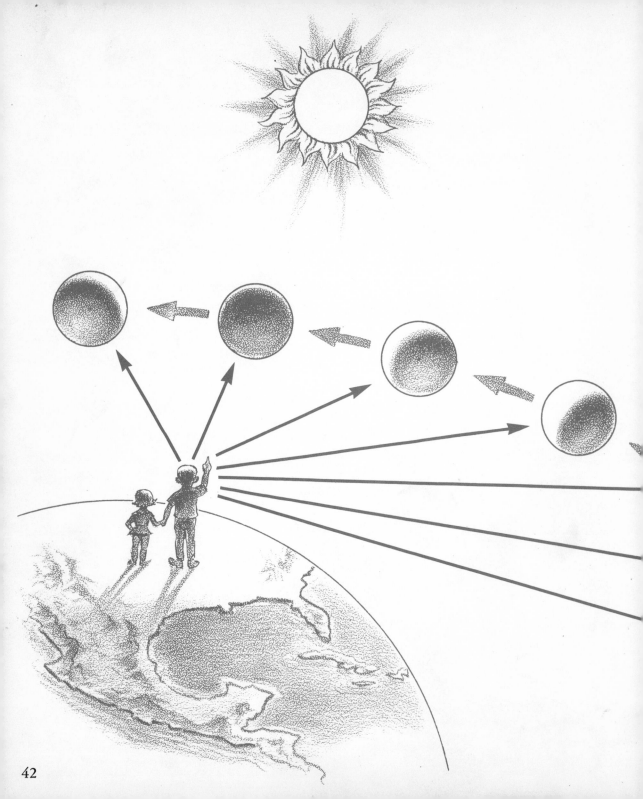

The shape of the moon seems to change a little
   from night to night.
But the shape doesn't really change.
As the moon circles the earth, we see more or
   less of the moon lighted up by the sun.

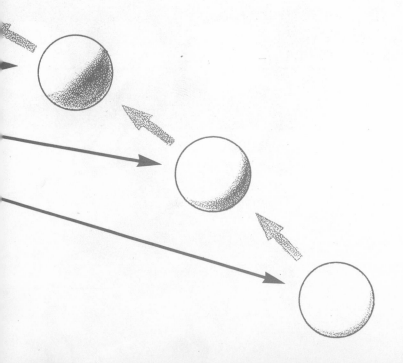

Sometimes the moon looks big and round.
Sometimes it looks like half a ball.
Sometimes we see only a slice of it.
And sometimes we do not see it at all.

It takes the moon about a month to go
completely around the earth.

When the moon is between the earth and the
sun, the side of the moon facing us is not
lighted up by the sun.

Because there is no light shining on the side
facing us, we cannot see the moon.

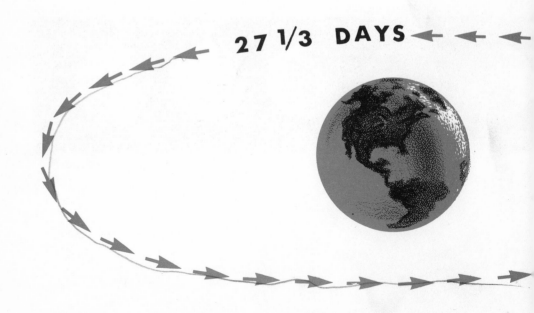

27 1/3 DAYS

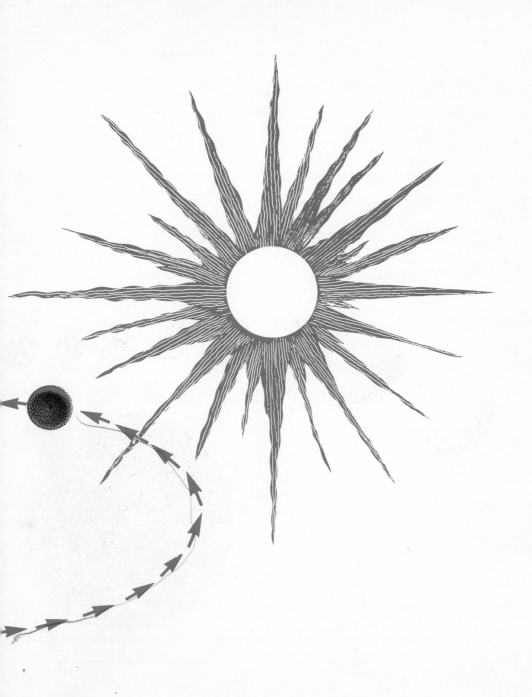

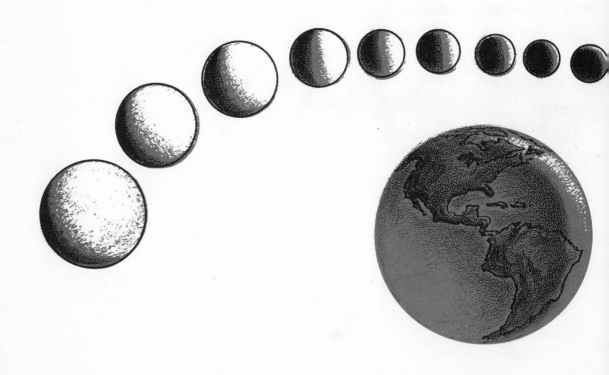

As it travels we see a little more of the moon.
Each night for two weeks we see more and
more of the lighted side of the moon.

Then the moon has made half its trip.
The earth is between the moon and the sun.
We see the whole face of the moon lighted up
　　by the sun.
We call this the full moon.

For the next two weeks, we see less and less of
the lighted side of the moon until we cannot
see it at all.
And the same thing happens the next month
and the next month and the next month.

There

Maybe some day, after men reach the moon,
they will blast off from a moon station and
reach another planet.

The LET'S FIND OUT Books

by Martha and Charles Shapp

LET'S FIND OUT ABOUT AIR

LET'S FIND OUT ABOUT ANIMAL HOMES

LET'S FIND OUT WHAT'S BIG AND WHAT'S SMALL

LET'S FIND OUT ABOUT CHRISTOPHER COLUMBUS

LET'S FIND OUT ABOUT COWBOYS

LET'S FIND OUT WHAT ELECTRICITY DOES

LET'S FIND OUT ABOUT FIREMEN

LET'S FIND OUT ABOUT OUR FLAG

LET'S FIND OUT ABOUT HOUSES

LET'S FIND OUT ABOUT INDIANS

LET'S FIND OUT ABOUT JOHN F. KENNEDY

LET'S FIND OUT WHAT'S LIGHT AND WHAT'S HEAVY

LET'S FIND OUT ABOUT ABRAHAM LINCOLN

LET'S FIND OUT ABOUT THE MOON

LET'S FIND OUT ABOUT POLICEMEN

LET'S FIND OUT ABOUT SAFETY

LET'S FIND OUT ABOUT SCHOOL

LET'S FIND OUT WHAT THE SIGNS SAY

LET'S FIND OUT WHAT'S IN THE SKY

LET'S FIND OUT ABOUT THE SUN

LET'S FIND OUT ABOUT THANKSGIVING

LET'S FIND OUT ABOUT THE UNITED NATIONS

LET'S FIND OUT ABOUT GEORGE WASHINGTON

LET'S FIND OUT ABOUT WATER

LET'S FIND OUT ABOUT WHEELS

and

LET'S FIND OUT ABOUT SPRING
LET'S FIND OUT ABOUT SUMMER
LET'S FIND OUT ABOUT FALL
LET'S FIND OUT ABOUT WINTER